D0923148

HANIMALS

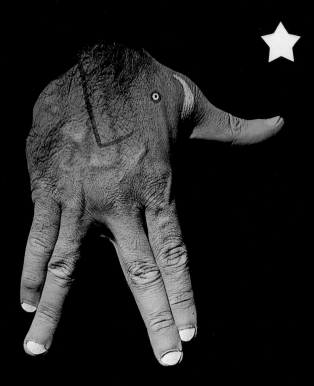

The Green Tiger Press

The idea and artistic realization of this book are by Mario Mariotti
Original color photographs by Roberto Marchiori

Green Tiger Press, Inc., San Diego, California 92101
Copyright © 1980 by La Nuova Italia Editrice S.p.A., Firenze
American edition copyright © 1982 by Green Tiger Press
First Edition • Ninth Printing
Library of Congress Catalog Card Number 84-144738
ISBN 0-914676-90-3
Printed and Bound in Singapore

BEFOREHAND

The ability to play with that which comes to hand—an acorn, a flower, a pebble, a puddle of water—involves the capacity to invent and transform.

Children today have many toys which structure play and leave little opportunity for creativity. We intend this book to be a beginning point for the imagination.

The human hand is of great symbolic importance. With it we touch others, we bless, we make, we pray, we speak, we greet, we nurture. Early men deliberately painted their hands on the walls of their caves.

This book attempts to direct us back to the hands' primacy and power. It tries to restore to us the wonder that those distant men felt when they looked at their hands.

The paint, water-based so that it can be easily removed, is applied to the hands with a brush, cotton, or by immersion.

Your creation's eyes can be glued into place. Doll's eyes are useful, as are buttons, marbles, game pieces, clay, or ping pong balls. Alternatively, eyes can be painted onto the hand.

If you wish to put on a play with your painted hands, you can use either a puppet theatre or the back of an armchair.

Do not hesitate to roll up your sleeves and plunge into the paint. Let your imagination flower. This book is only a starting place. You can bring a whole world of new animals to life.

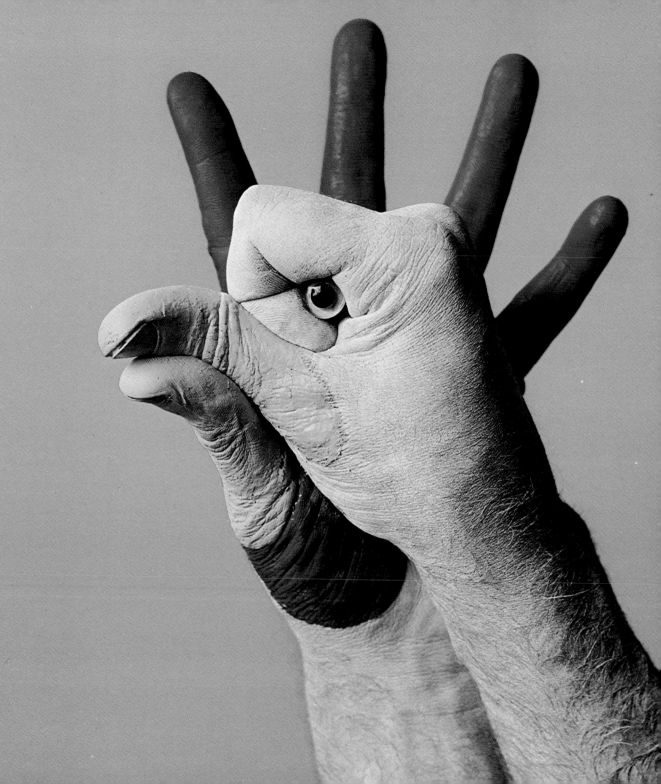

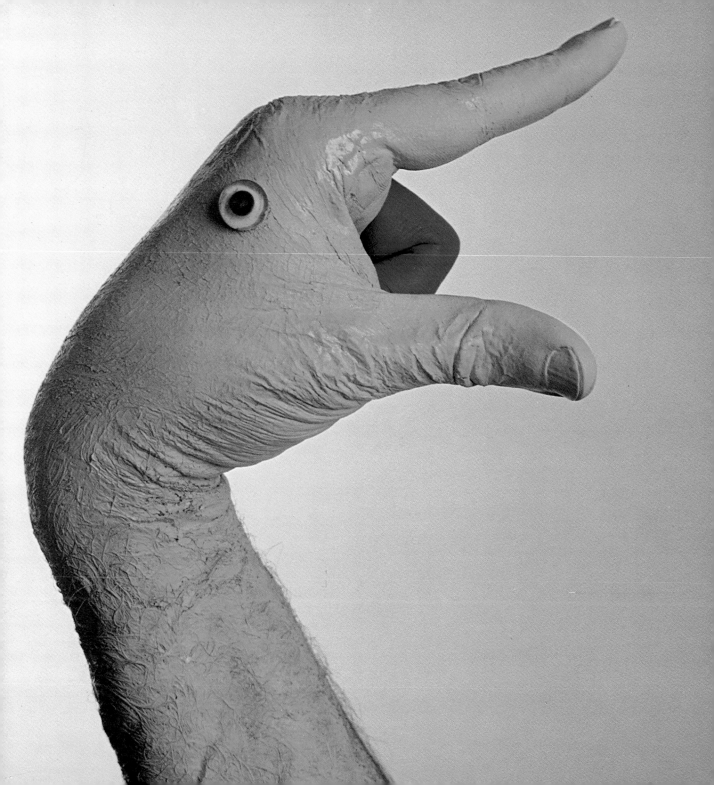

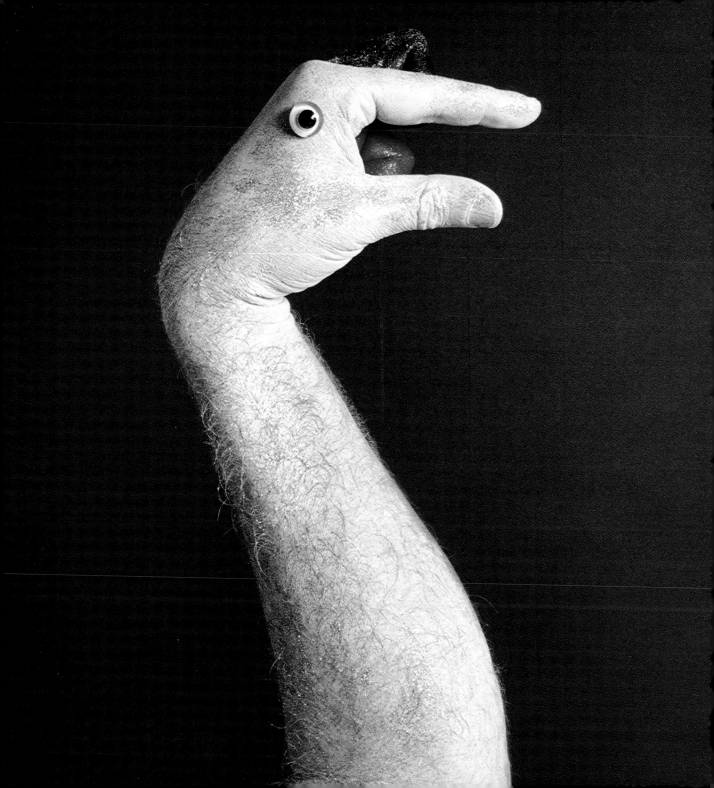

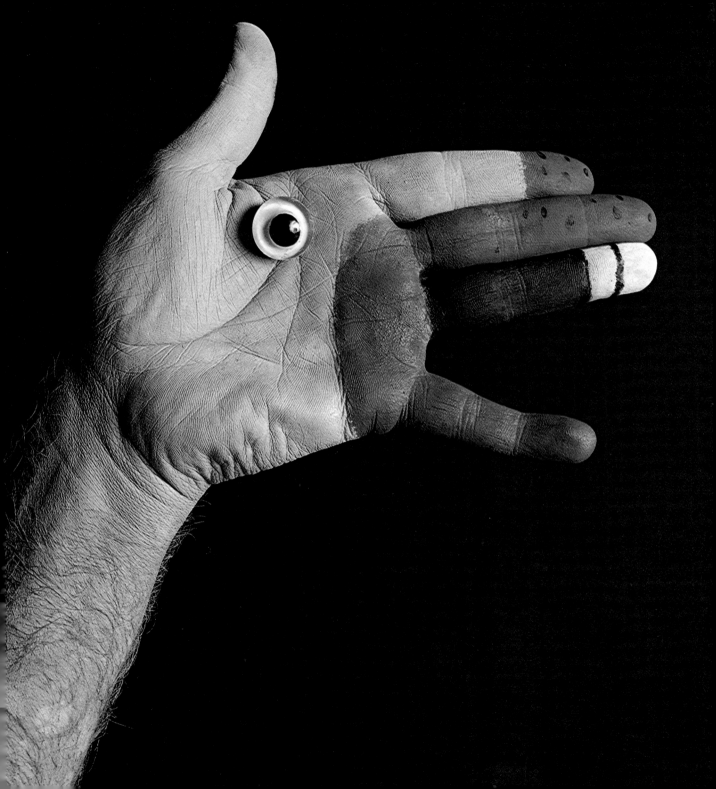

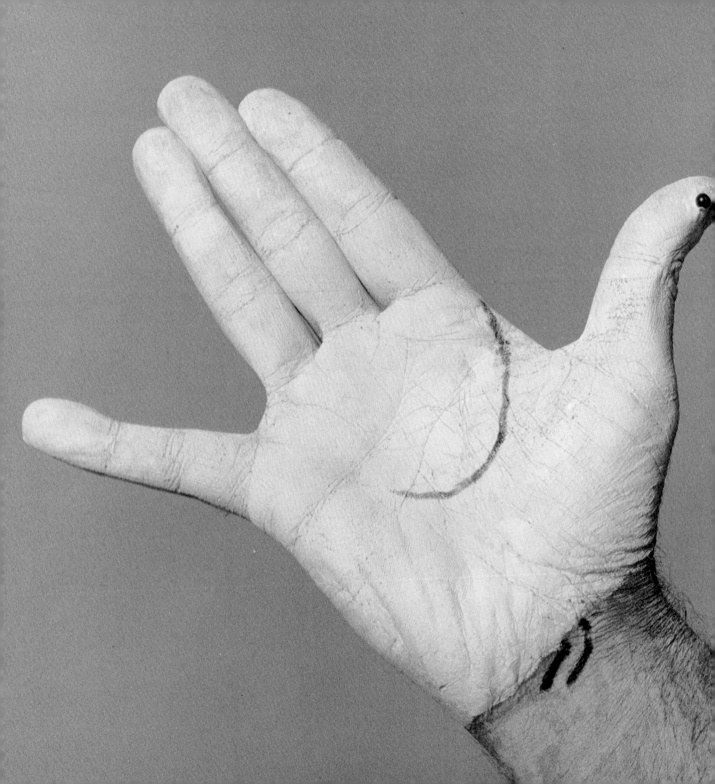

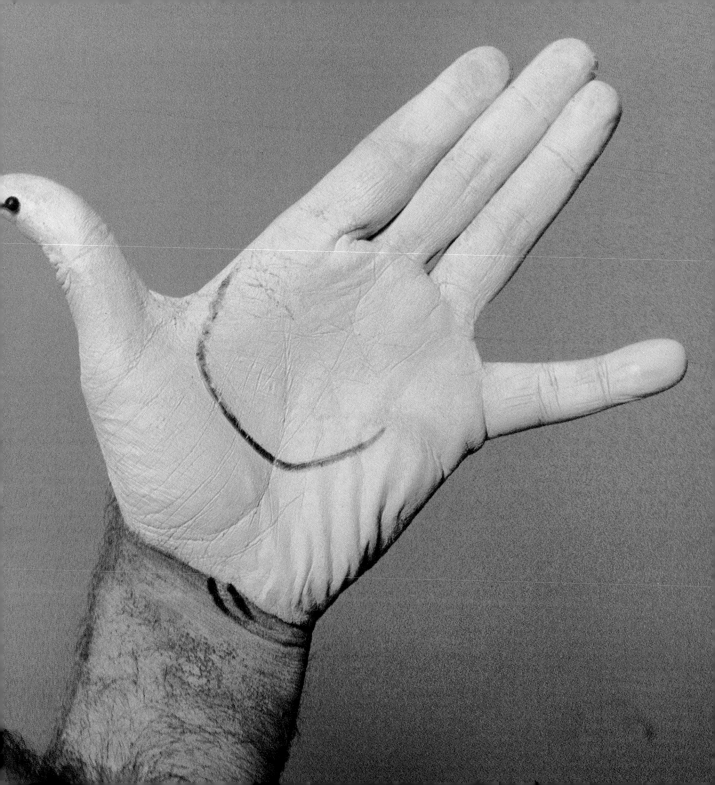

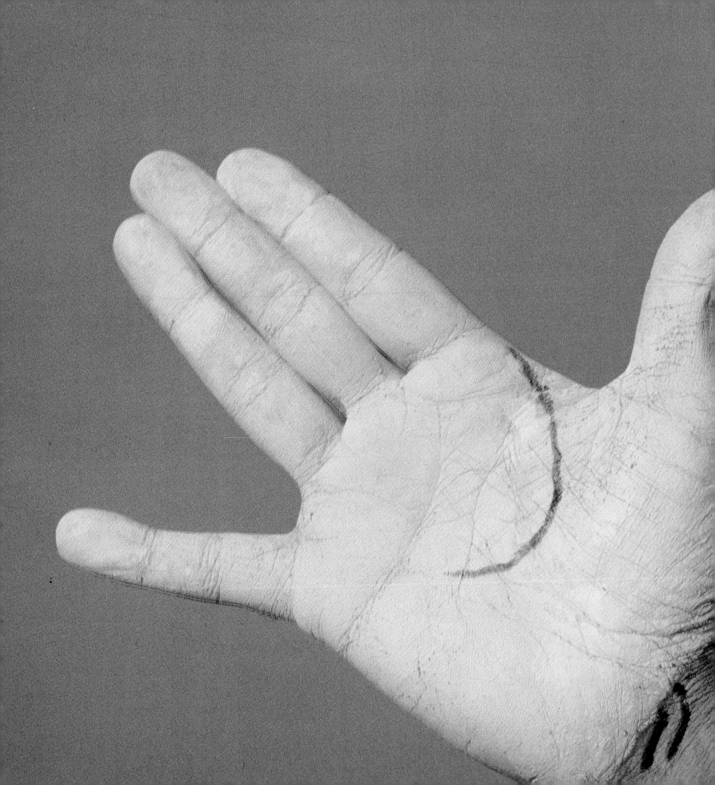

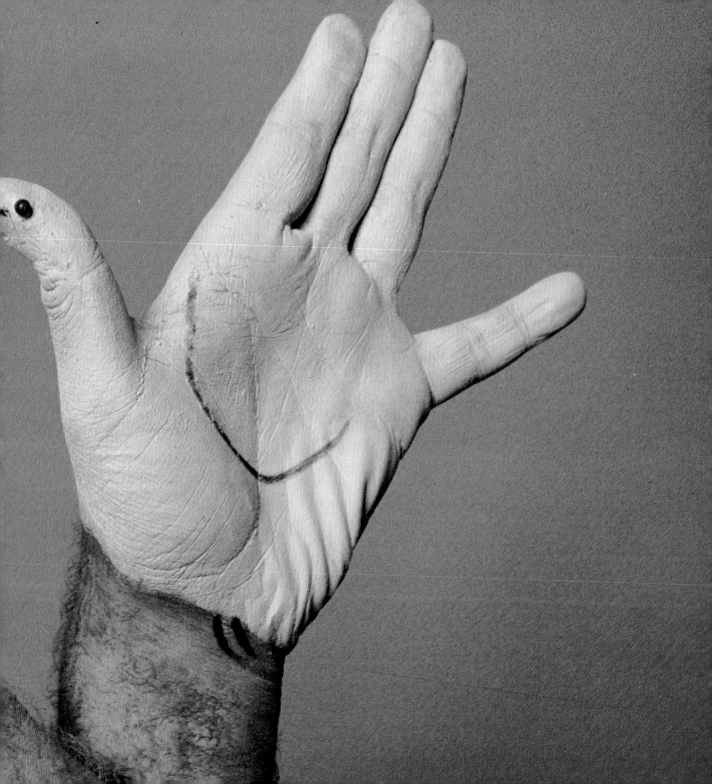

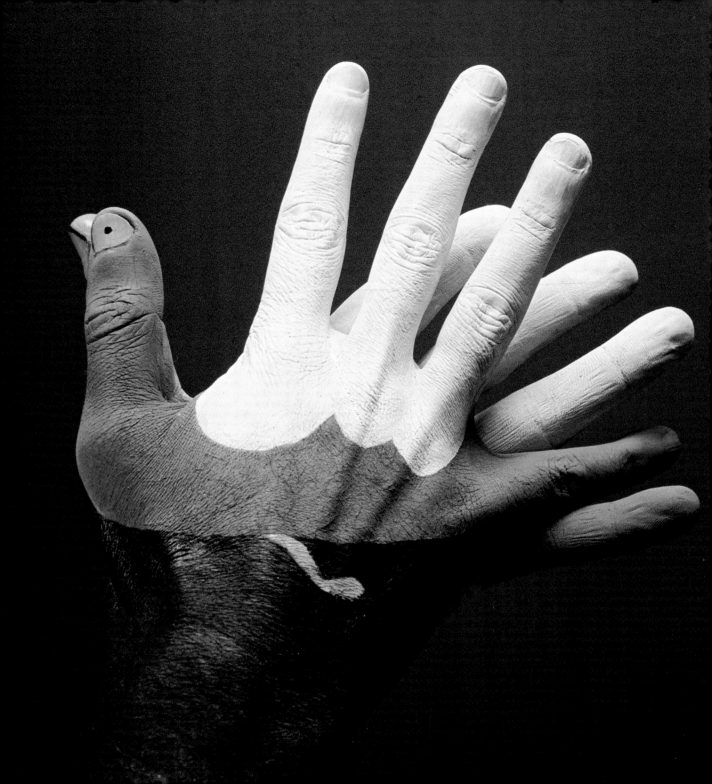

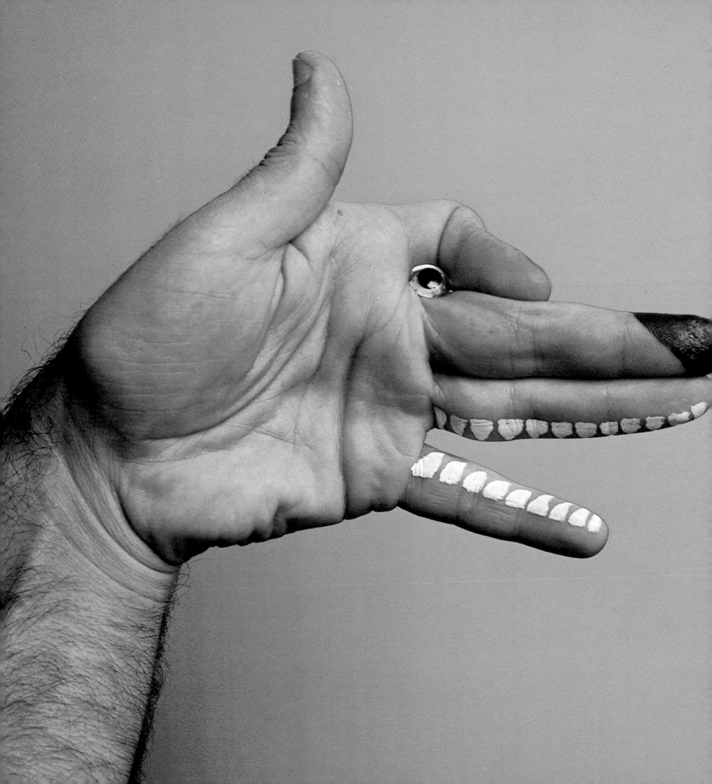

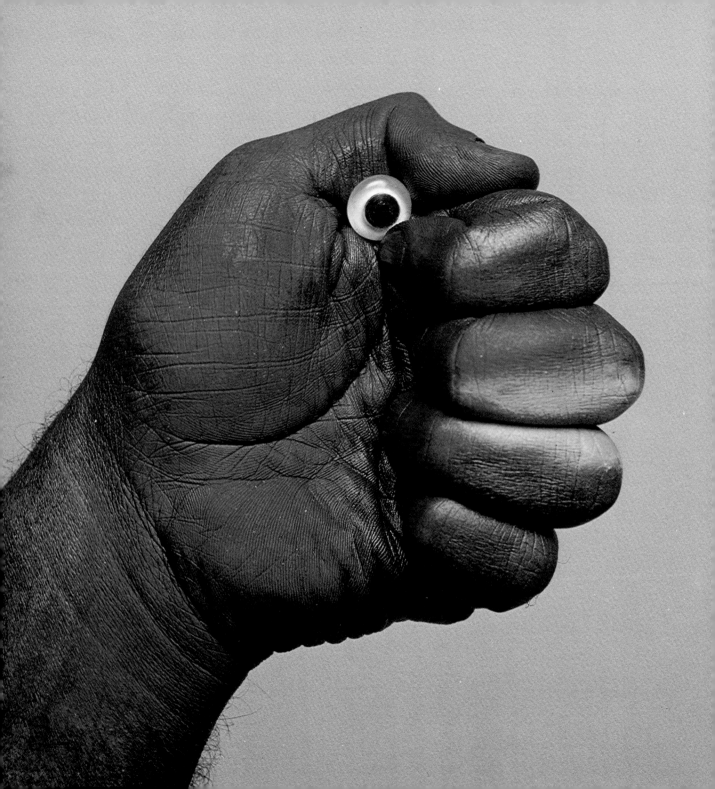

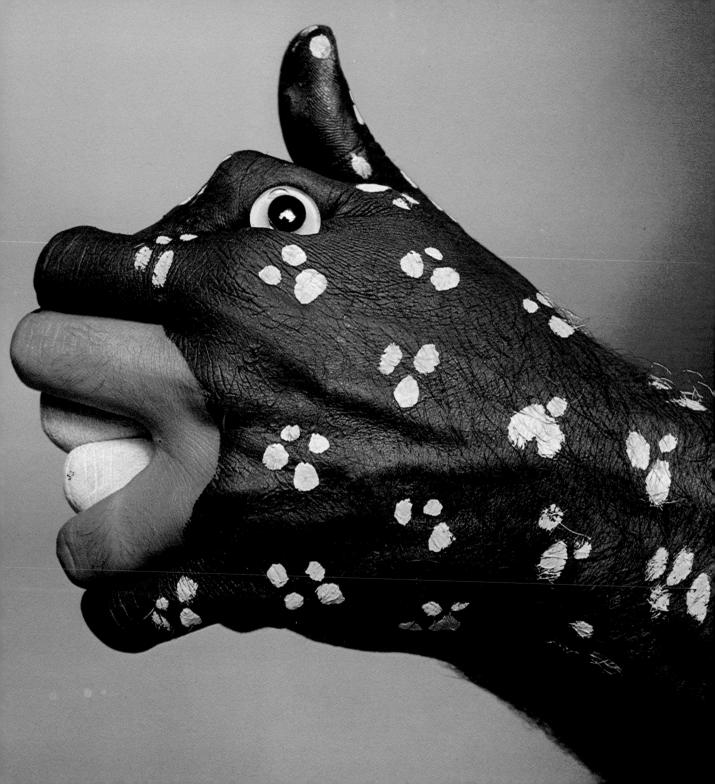

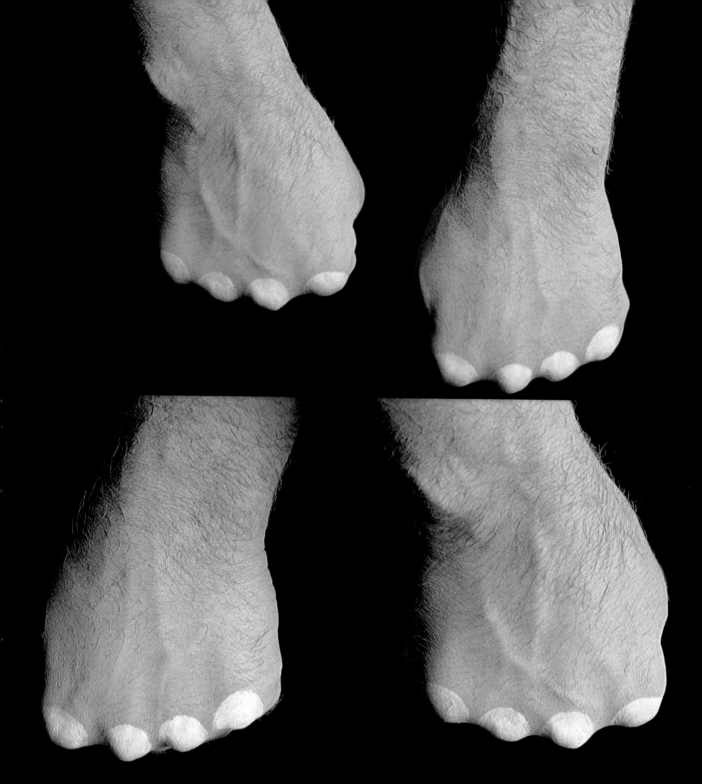

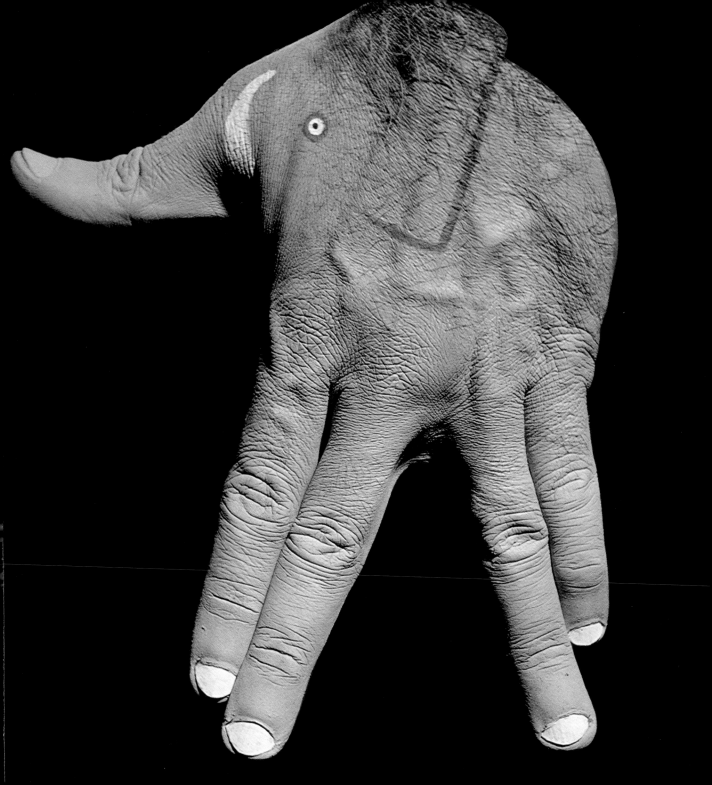

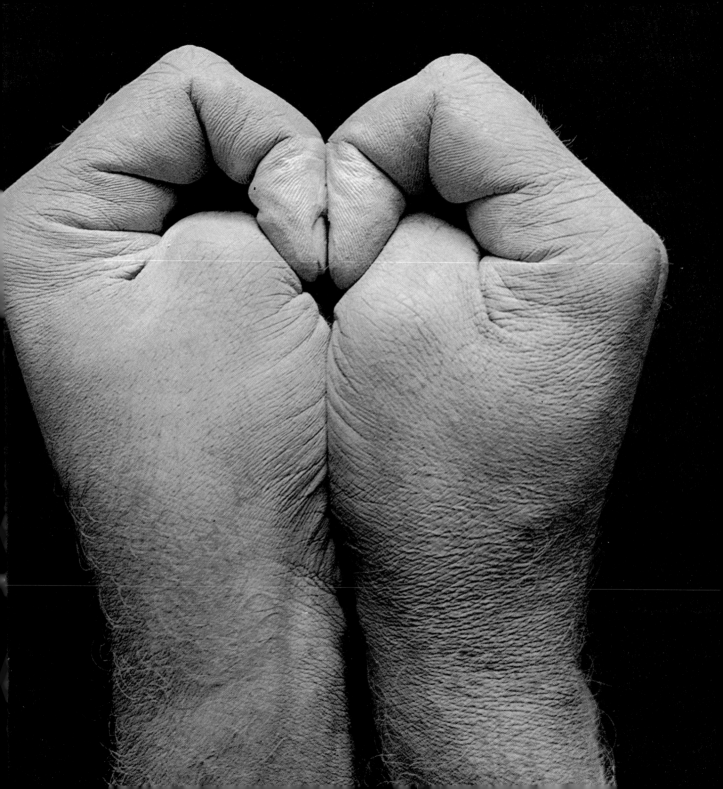

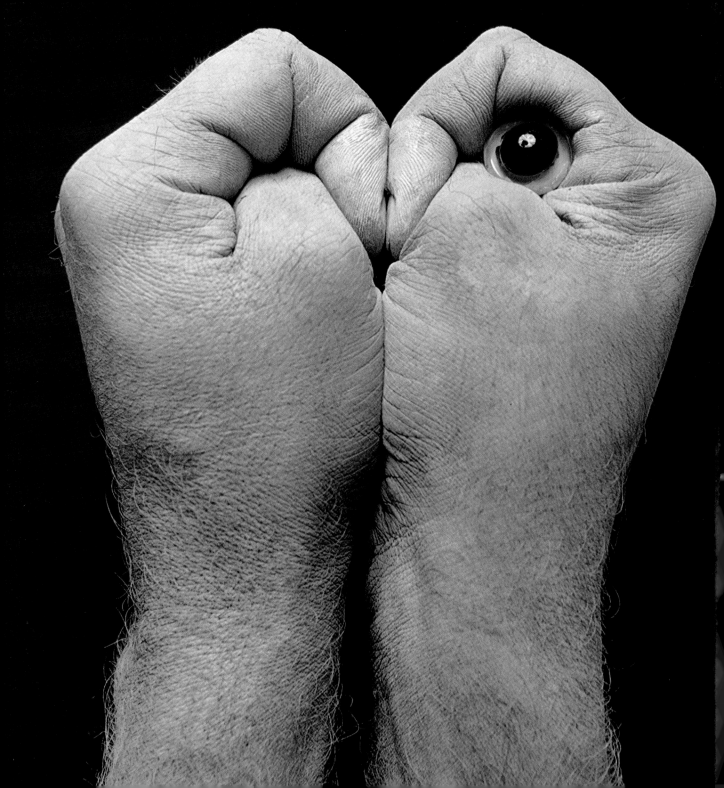